veto my vote

volume twelve

pamela fields

S.H.E. PUBLISHING, LLC

For information contact :

info@shepublishingllc.com

www.shepublishingllc.com

Book Cover and Title Page design by Michelle Phillips of
CHELLD3 3D VISUALIZATION AND DESIGN

ISBN :

978-1-953163-52-3 (paperback)

First Edition : October 2022

10 9 8 7 6 5 4 3 2 1

Preface

I came from a long generation of ex-slaves. My history and soul is all boughed up with slave time stories. My heart beat slavery, wrist still feel where once chains prevented my access to come and go, my free will and freedom of choice was in someone else hands. I can smell slavery even though the stench of it is gone yet lingers evidence blowing in the winds. So, just to assure my stand in this very controversial matter; no man should have the right, or the say so over that of a woman. But rather the woman should examine herself. In the very definition of a woman, the right to bare children should be her aim, her goal and a right no man, woman, law, man made law should take.

Conditions make women consider killing her unborn child. In this book I consider these women as Mom (Mom or Murderer).

PAMELA FIELDS

Fear of the unknown and unjust treatment of single moms are a few of the conditions that make women consider abortion. Not only is it unjust, but it is also not easy. Hats off and a bow to women like my mother, having four children by age 20 and our father walked off, tempted by the devil dressed as a woman, and his own lust.

When I lost my children in a court of law, I felt like a mom in a nightmare. The one where she takes her child to a shopping mall and loses them in the mall. Perhaps a brief second when she lets go of their hand and they wander off. But the incident is played over and over in vivid images of that moment, every time she closes her eyes. Now fast forward ahead twenty years for everyone to see, that that was not the best move/decision. Everyone sees but the judge who awarded it so.

CONTENTS

veto my vote

volume twelve

pamela fields

Introduction

If this book can save just one child, it would have served its purpose.

It is not what the government says about the rights of an individual, you got to know that God knows, and He see your heart. That the only thing He is asking you is to love, even that unborn child. Love is a strong emotion and love is heart felt even to the uterus.

I cannot tell women what to do with their bodies. God give men the ability to choose, and while he can force a people to serve Him, He gives us free choice. The will to choose to serve Him, and in doing that, we choose to love, showing the fruits of the spirit, being kind to each other, even family, even that unborn child. So, if there is an over abundance of abortions, perhaps it's the church we should point a finger at. Perhaps the church need to do a better job of teaching, showing and giving love. I am talking about the kind of love that spreads, that is contagious, and the kind of sentiment that is felt, seen, that touches the heart, is apologetic and forgiving.

Where people go wrong is that they try to make people do things their way. Because you don't believe as I do, then we are immediately at war? I must physically fight you because you don't share my opinion? That is what is wrong; the fight, the immediate threat that out weights everything, conflict, and considering you an enemy because you don't agree with me, the void of common sense that seems to be thrown out the window.

In the life of a Christian there should be a stance that shows others the joyous life in serving God. And when a woman, my friend, sister or anybody believes that the only way out for her is to abort her unborn child, then I have to know and realize that some battles will be lost. Life on earth is equivalent to a wagging war. The one enemy that we all have is that against the evil forces of the Devil. I write this book with the purpose of showing young women that turning the pages of life, having an unplanned child is not the end; yet having to abort that child is not the end neither.

So, to the pro-choice, to the pro-life, I totally agree. But to the cause of your fight, Veto My Vote.

VETO MY VOTE

1 | Life Lessons

I look at the children of the times we are presently living in, and I wonder why they are so angry, full of attitude, and disrespect. They are full of rejection, lies, hurts from the past that taunts them sorely. They have been misguided by it and the ugly truths is now being revealed.

I am no psychologist, I have no Ph.D., but what I do is study people. I have matured and seasoned over the years. I listen to my elders and my mother. Old people have a lot to say if you take the time to listen. They are full of wisdom and life's experiences.

2 |

Games Played with Life

Put three cups on a table,

Under one of the cups,

place a shinning silver dollar,

Switch the cups around and around

Now choose the cup with the

shinning silver dollar under it.

Many times, we choose wrong.

Because we are led by our feelings,

and feelings of the flesh.

Know it all feelings

It hurts or will hurt

And feelings of just because.

Dreams of a Master Killer

I wonder
what types of dreams
President Putin has at night.

A man
who starts a war
with a country with a just because attitude.

Sure,
his dreams are to win the war
against the country of Ukraine,

But just like any greedy individual, it will never be enough.
He dreams to conquer the world, just like the villain in most
evil movies.

PAMELA FIELDS

A walking,
talking,
breathing evil.

People of old
used to talk about when they knew
it was going to be a war in the land.

They were able to tell by their wisdom,
and most would judge it by the number of male children
being born in a specific amount of time.

Wisdom
speaks
when others do not.

And even now,
when our male children are being destroyed, killed,
murdered and is upsetting even the voice of wisdom.

4 | *Precious Pearls*

Women,
young women with those precious pearls.
You do have control of your bodies.

You make decisions everyday
about who you give your pearls to.

You lure men in and out of your bed,
This is the time to think about it before it's too late.

Chastity belts
Chaperone
Common Sense
Either one will do...

Would that man make a good husband, father?
Do you even know the man you have chosen to lie down with?

Giving away your pearls is a precious part of life
you should consider very seriously before you do.

5 | The Price of Sin

The Lord God commanded the man...

of the tree of the knowledge of good and evil,

thou shalt not eat of it...

Gen. 2:16, 17

For the first sin,

God spoke to His people

God said unto the serpent:

Upon thy belly shalt thou go,

and dust shalt thou eat all the days of thou life.

VETO MY VOTE

Unto the woman,

God said:

In sorrow thou shalt bring forth children.

Unto the man, God said:

In the sweat of thy face shalt thou eat bread,

till thou return unto the ground.

Gen. 3:14,16,19

That is God's law,

not mine,

not no law maker,

God's law according to Genesis.

Not Safe in The Womb

I think about the babies of the world,
who God takes back.

They leave this world at such an early age in a short life.
The beauty of life,
they never get to experience on this realm.

Yet in peace, they take their wings
And their little spirits take off
Reporting back to the spirit giver.

Turning their backs on this cruel, cruel, cold world.

Reporting back saying,
"Eve," meaning the mother of all living, (Gen. 3:20)
"rejected me."

So, truly, truly to not want a child is to deny the sperm
an opportunity to squeeze itself into the oval
membrane and enter the walls of the egg which bears
life opportunities.

7 |

Should It Be Overturned?

Somebody's got to do it,
> Mother and nurture children.
> Mothers trying to go on strike.
> True mothers, are you going to be a player or
>> Continue to side on the lines of
>> Doubt and regret?

Let the real mothers push forth
> Why should science get in the way of what
>> Was meant to be natural?

Let the real mothers push forth
> Why should politics get in the way when
>> The mother in us know the right thing to do.

Surrogates and egg donors, artificial insemination, and vitro
fertilization replacing sex, a real act of love, birthing forth a
child, the symbol of that love.

One thing that I do know is that too many children are being pushed out of the womb, born, growing up to be full of hate.

Don't take my word for it, ask any teacher stuck with a classroom full of angry children because mothers are on "strike." A reflection of this anger and attitude, void of self-will and self-determination, because this anger has no voice and shows out in self-destructive flare ups.

Love, hope, peace and even kindness; it's not demonstrated in the home. Not when mothers work till the wee hours and lie down with Tom one week and Harry the next, then to find out she is pregnant. These are the mothers who will push out every one of these children, (none having the same father). Come on, we all know someone like this. Not planning or being able to afford a roof over her own head. Living with the mercy of another's willingness to give, to help, but at what price? We are talking about children learning to hate from the womb. Them coming to school with attitudes, hurts, problems, then growing up with inner pain, a hurt from the inside.

People growing up with hurt and inner pain make bad citizens. Mainly because, how do you express all this hurt? You express it with hate, violence, rage and void of inward peace.

True mothers, we can and should correct all of this. Stop having children out of wed lock. When you date, make sure he is the right person for you. Be true and truthful and expect it in return. Mistakes will be made, but when you lie down with a man, know that he will do right by you. I'm reminded of the meaning behind shotgun weddings.

VETO MY VOTE

Building strong families, accent on building, require a man, a woman and then the children. James Brown, father of soul said it best, "This is a man's world, but it wouldn't be nothing without a woman."

Roe v Wade, should it be overturned? The case that made history March 28, 1970 with claims regarding women that:
- Described a lack of protection for single mothers
- Employment policies required pregnant women to take leave of absence or quit their jobs, etc.

You decide... and when you do, do it because of your true inward you. Stand up and be a woman. Taking on the role and responsibilities of a woman and not just that, coming to the table with pride and dignity. Not shame, disgust, regret and a life's secret.

Our children are being raised void of real mothers, that real connection and why we don't have successful candidates for the office of president.

Our world is threatened because mothers are away from their post. Your role as mother is more important than you could ever know.

8 |

A Call for Real Mothers

This is the era where the call for real mothers can be
heard in a distant cry. Help wanted signs posted in
the door window, on street corners and in every for-
hire agency, the cry for mothers call.

No experience necessary,
just a willingness to learn and

The time necessary to fulfill the post.

Could it be that the real moms
are becoming extinct?

Where have they all gone?
Are they on strike?

9 |

Conversation of a future gathering of moms:

Science done figured out a way to take the pain out of laboring, so the only real work is the discomfort of carrying the child in the belly for nine months. So, the very rich and modestly income society will not disfigure their bodies even to bring their own children into the world. The conversation goes as this mother is holding her own child, birthed with the use of a surrogate…

* * *

"I remember when women had children only through labor pain. Where a doctor assisted the birth and sometimes had to cut a woman down there. Then sewed her back up. Women would cry out and yell for hours in pain during the process. My mama told me that some women even died during the process of delivery."

I am reminded of the movie about the life of Moses. His mother (one who raised him) was sister to the Pharoah of Egypt. Here is a perfect example of the kind of motherhood we are evolving into. In the movie, Moses didn't know he was born of Jewish descent. Yet he possessed the character that demonstrated he had more integrity as a Jew than that of any Pharoah, no matter the riches. This is not any old movie; it is based on the Bible.

* * *

How many times in Early Childhood Education study do we discover that the early years are the most important years in a child's life. I am persuaded to believe that also mean the years of development, as a mother carries her child, what she eats, listens to, her encounters and conversations with the child's father all play a significant role in this child's character.

* * *

Moses true mother (what we would call his surrogate today) was allowed to nurse him. Can you imagine her singing to him in the Hebrew language; sweet talk and voices of direction, clues and instructions of future things to come.

VETO MY VOTE

The conversation continues from the child being in the womb, and him listening to the same heartbeat. There is no sense of fooling ourselves, the surrogate and birth mother are one in the same. No amount of money can change that. No court of law can change that, paying a surrogate is a form of legal bribery, a ransom if you please, in my forefather's day it was called slavery, to buy a child.

10

Rights of The Unborn Child

And what of the rights of the unborn child,
Who advocates for them?

How many adopted children have you seen or heard of
To grow up and earnestly look for their birth mother.

Many angry through life,
never really knowing who they really are
Not really fitting in.

And parents, who may lose a child
In the process of this mixed-up world,
Seek to find that child.

Even mothers who abort a child is taunted
By thoughts of what if, never really knowing
The outcome of what this child's life would have been:

VETO MY VOTE

Success, stardom, rich, smart, athletic,
Especially when it seems that her other children
Never reach their full potential.

11 |

The Shame of Sin Is Crying

Crying out and making a noise:

A noise that screams when our population is dying by the thousands;

Plagues and pandemics, mass shootings, gun banging, baby killing, natural disasters, suicides and accidents.

A noise, when mass murders repeat itself again and again and within a month from the last occurrence.

A noise where the division of a nation has nothing to do with right or wrong, but because of crimes in law which is the true reason for the division.

VETO MY VOTE

A noise which intends to be heard, which cannot be ignored.

A noise, making babies cry and cover their ears.

Noise brought on by sirens, police cars, and ambulance.

Noise reported on network news, good news, dull by comparison.

And everyone walking around wearing skeletons, skulls and cross bones like it's the latest style.

12 | Young Men, Young Men, Yes You!

Young men, young men
You better treat that woman right.

You may not understand your true worth.
Loving the women then leaving them,
Playing the game, only to misuse your true love.

Love her
Leave her
Play on her
Did you ever take her serious at all?

VETO MY VOTE

Young and strong men in your youth
But did you know, young men grow old?
Did you know they get sick?
And they get weak.

Did you know
That's when you begin to think
On the love you lost.

Like losing a million dollars
Keys to a Hot Rod
Or the loss of a warm home.

Something, that love that you had
The one that loved you back
The one that you never invested time
Now it is gone.

Love her
Leave her
Play on her
Did you ever take her serious at all?
Now she is gone.

13 |
Combatting Crime

For every rape –
Jennie In a Bottle appears,
Removing the sting of hurt and danger
And releasing in its stead a willing Jennie
Giving the rapist something back in return.
This would be an eternal ring,
That fits perfectly around the penis
And tightens when the urge to rape
Again develops.
For the word of God says, "As a man
Thinketh in his heart, so is he."

For every shoot'em up –
Cat and mouse chase like unto Tom and Jerry
The cat comes out to shoot the mouse
But everyone knows that Tom and Jerry

VETO MY VOTE

Are really friends, so the mouse calls Tom
Who chase away the other cats that's playing rough
Also, Tom knows people in high places
And whispers breathe of exchange in prayer.

For every thief –
Many of us know there are two
Kinds of thieves/robbery
  1) The robbery of greed
  2) The robbery of Robin Hood
Let us examine closely the kind of thief you are.
The type of robbery you have committed
What did you gain from it?
Did any other gain anything?
Does this robbery entitle you to punishment or reward?
So, the one is a robbery intended in secret quarters.
The other shared outwardly amongst the needy.

Crimes of passion –
Crimes taken too far
Please, please reveal when enough is enough
People who do the wrong thing just for the love of it.
Taking it too far in the wrong direction to the point
That they hurt others in the process.
Nothing that a good dose of Jesus couldn't solve
Medicine that heals.

14 | Bad Seed

There is a seed that manages to find its way to the birth canal

And penetrate the egg in a fight to be born.

This seed comes into the world
with mess-causing-issues.

Getting anyone involved geeked up and upset.

Bringing stress to a point of insanity, a boiling point.

Yet the seed makes it into the world.

The attraction that draws these seeds to the egg
Lust, nasty and a lack, A void of real love.

15 | Veto Is My Vote

VETO IS MY VOTE BECAUSE YOUR CHILD IS PART OF your team. When you come into this world, you have nothing. Your child, family, team helps you build an empire, a future, your brand. That child believes everything you say, even your lies. But be very careful, you should never lie to a child, cause when he finds the truth, you are who he takes it out on. So, this child is part of your team. A part of you. When you give that child away, abort it, or simply ignore him, you give yourself away. A part of you is missing, would you do that? Have you ever heard where a child may bring out something in you, the best in you, bring you out of a dark place? While sometimes we need that child to complete us.

WE MAY FIND OUR LIFE'S ANSWERS, BUT HIDING behind lies and secrets puts us further behind when we won't learn lessons from the mistakes we make in life.

16 |

Future Conversations:

FUTURE CONVERSATIONS OF THE RICH: I got my surrogate to do it. (Meaning, whatever she doesn't feel like doing surrogate will do it for a dollar.) Remind me of the old plantation nannies. Raised all the children but not her own. She was however able to bring them things, maybe some old hand-me-downs given to her by her mistress. Like the surrogate, she'll be able to pay her bills, put food on the table, but what percentage of her quality time will be rendered to her own children, family? Let your children see you pick up a book and read, enjoy meals together, even difficult task, let them see you getting through it. Sing, smile, conversating as you participate.

Why, **ABORTION RIGHTS DON'T BENEFIT THE POOR AT ALL,** but the very rich. Planned pregnancy is what this is all about. Another source of control. In a day where everybody's jumping in and out of bed with everyone that's not their spouse. In a day where no one wants to get caught or caught up. The real control should be about controlling whom you're sleeping with, whom you're having sex with, who's in your bed, control that!

THE SAFEST PLACE IN THE WORLD should be a mother's womb. Now for a little animal instinct sex, everything else gets placed out of proportion.

17 |

Using the Language

To pray, adultery, fornicate, sexual sin, the Holy Bible **is G**od's written word, giving us, His people, His children instruction on living here on Earth. We tip-toe around these words. We refrain from using these words like they are bad words, when in fact the words which are bad words, we choose to use in our daily vocabulary. We laugh about it when our children pick the word up and they use it in their daily vocabulary. There comes a time in life when we must teach right from wrong, when lessons must be learned, when we must slow down and go through something so that we will learn the lessons that come with it.

I'll tell you though, this abortion issue has become a win, win for men. Win number one, he gets to have all your cookies. Win number two, your talk about getting rid of the evidence, the child conceived during your rendezvous has relieved him of any obligation to be responsible to the child he has fathered.

18 | Mass Killing

Buried secrets of a criminal,
is this where our society is at?

No wonder
unknown terrors plague our cities.

Danger in the city amidst gun shootings,
carjackings and other woes.

How much more is there
than the danger in the womb.

The school shootings,
how horrific to take the life of all those children.

Sadden society
by the tragic events.

National news reports the tragedy
as people gather around the TV
or read the newspaper of the horrible acts.

PAMELA FIELDS

First thoughts,
then second thoughts flash through your mind.

Minor victims fall prey
to the mad shooters.

Officers of the law file into the school building
and take the shooter out.

But what of the falling victims of the womb?
As countless Moms seeking to keep a secret untold.

The secret in their womb,
a live growth, childbearing tissue,
breathing through you his Mom,
and supposed protector, a process, a development
until the child is breathing on his/her own.

Who can say what this child's future would be,
because each of us are here
for a God intended purpose?

This too should be an event which saddens society,
cause it too is tragic.

19 | Cause and Effect

It is very clear to see that something is wrong with these children. There is a void, something missing which no one can explain because physically they are fine. It's the emotions, the social ability, they're sad and easily aroused to anger. It's like they're walking around in a world by themselves. No one to talk to, no one to share their thoughts, happy times or sad times. It's like their best friend (BF) never made it to the planet. An expectancy which never happened, creating a void in a very deep place. We have all experienced having a best friend. Looking back, what would you have done if that best friend was not there for you? Well, these children are walking around on the Earth void of an experience we all should experience in life.

Even women who desire to be married and that right mate never shows up. Political arenas, where all the participants are crooks. Moms are disallowing key players from entering the realm of the Earth's atmosphere, they are acting like "gods" when they reverse things that are supposed to happen naturally. It's like stopping the rain from falling in spring. There is a thing called cause and effect, the science of how things work, how they are supposed to work. And because Mom disallowed her child to come into the world, someone lost a best friend, someone lost a lover/husband/wife. Someone, the world lost that invention, that next president, that doctor who would have saved a life and possessed the cure to a decease we are dealing with today. And we, as a society are paying for it when we must witness mass murders and the ill effects of lonely hearts and secrets, and the horrors of wicked schemes. We pay when all our politicians are old, we pay when this diseased plagued world still searches for an answer. Answers that were sucked out of its Mom's womb. And because that happened, this was affected.

20 | Farewell Cycle

Because that lover, husband or wife was not permitted,

did not gain access, was disallowed,
released into the eternity of the after – thoughts,
we will never get access to that soul's lineage,
patrilineage or matrilineage.

Like a generation swiped from the world

like you would swipe a debit or credit card,
subtracting from it to pay on an account.
Leaving behind a negative balance against the equation of time.
Adding up to this big mess which we have in the world today.
Nobody told you that, that one little child,
that baby could make a difference to help balance the book of
broken homes, secrets and deep seeded anger.

Secrets which need to be discovered

in order that a lesson will be learned,
hence the beginning of growth.

That learned lesson then helps to prevent others

when taught through the lenses of the receiver.
Those who witnessed and learned
and not only that but gained insight
that they may teach and help
to straighten this broken system.

Farewell to a great nation of unwanted,

untold, unclaimed gifts, yet innocent babies.

21 | The Author of Life

DO GOD GET A VOTE? In the heat of passion, he was there. Can God bless you through an unwanted pregnancy? To say that it cannot be done is to say that He can only bless you through a wanted pregnancy. Or that through your choice of which pregnancy to keep, then you have control of your blessings. That's ludicrous, slaphappy hilarious.

YOU SEE HE IS THE GIVER OF LIFE and He takes a life also. That's why it is such a sin to take someone's life and justly, the Laws of the Earth provides a penalty for such an act.

GOD, WHO GIVES LIVES AND TAKES IT, has not granted approval when you give back to Him a child, for whatever reason you think you cannot keep. In society it is considered pretty rude to give back a gift. In this case, we, people don't even know what gift we are giving back. What if the mother of Jesus had given back our Lord and Savior? "Here God, I don't want this gift."

I'M REMINDED OF A YOUNG MOTHER, she being young, already with three children, found herself to be pregnant again. Now, I don't know the circumstances that surrounded the facts of how or why that pregnancy came about, but she told me the story of how she took that child in her womb to God. Crying, praying, begging and pleading, in a heat of emotions seeking direction.

GOD ALREADY KNEW THE WHOLE STORY, and that she would go on to have two more children after that encounter. Him seeing her predicament – a difficult, unpleasant or embarrassing situation, took the child. She had no need to abort, yet He answered her cry.

MANY OF US NEVER GO TO HIM with our predicaments. We choose to handle it ourselves. Which is why there has to be a difference between unborn babies who die at His hands and ones who die at the hands of MOM (Mom or Murderer).

I'M REMINDED OF ANOTHER MOM, my own, who choose not to end my life using what was then known as a wire coat hanger, a self-induced abortion. After seeing people she knew and respected, even loved go through this horrible and hideous procedure, at the tender age of 16, she chose not to venture into what seemed like a dangerous and life risking act. Thank you, Mama. My absence in this world may not have caused such a ripple, but say that to my siblings and the many I've come to be a role model. Say that to my children who lack cousins because their Aunt and Uncle, my siblings never had children. Say that to the young children I teach and to the many who have found me to be a true friend. Thank you, God for my life.

Looking to Jesus the author and finisher of our faith...
Heb. 12:2

22 | Enjoy the Eggs

I broke open two eggs, I preceded to springle salt and pepper in them. I cut up some American Cheese and added it to the yolk and then poured in a teaspoon of milk. I stirred the egg yolk mixture all together, added some butter into the skillet, poured the mixture in and cooked. I stirred the mixture and stirred, then decided within myself I didn't want the eggs after all. I continued to stir until the scrambled eggs with cheese added were well done. I poured the cooked eggs into the bowl, grabbed my coffee then sat down and ate my breakfast. What I saw as I was preparing this meal, my built-up anxiety and predetermination of how I felt about this meal turned out to be pretty delicious. If you would have seen me, it would not be needed to say, how much I enjoyed the eggs.

23 |
The Wheat vs. The Tares

*God's army is dying at the hands of pretenders.
Pretenders of being innocent, pretenders of being true
Christians, pretenders of being righteous while hiding the
secrets of shame, and murder.*

*We are living in a world where the devour is cleverly
sprinkling seeds of wickedness throughout the world.
While seeds of God are being aborted and rejected in the
Earth.*

*There is a scripture that says, Let the tares and the wheat
grow together. Today we're seeing more and more tares
grow alone, and eventually show itself for all to see its
worth.*

VETO MY VOTE

Let both grow together until the harvest: and in the time of harvest I will say to the reapers, gather ye together first the tares, and bind them in bundles to burn them: but gather the wheat into my barn. **Matt. 13:30**

24 | Where Does Hate Come From?

...An age-old question. Babies don't come into the world having hatred and knowing how to hate. They come into the world as an empty slate. They learn hatred from a lack of love and the presence of hate around them. They learn from precepts and examples of how to dislike and to hate others for the void of love in their lives even in the womb. Rejection grows into anger and anger into rage and inwardly hate evolves and shows itself from its actions and words.

25 | Amnesty

Amnesty is the act of an authority by which pardon is granted to a large group of individuals. A general pardon for offenses.

There is nothing the unborn fetus has done to be pardoned for, yet they have been sentenced to the most brutal and unjust sentence. There is nothing the unborn fetus has done. No offenses at the unborn child's hand. But amnesty is what is needed. Amnesty to bring pardon on the heads and hearts of those who offenses lay heavily.

To God who is the authority of all mankind, pardon me for the unborn child, killed at my request. For the blood and blame on my hands. Pardon me for the thoughts and plans of cover up and yes, even for thinking as a little "god" like I'm in control of life. Pardon me for allowing my life to get out of hand, for the sin of fornication and/or adultery. Grant me pardon and remove the stain of guilt which lies at my door. Break this nasty habit everywhere and cause women to live by a higher standard, one of respect of self and that families may be built through us.

Grant me amnesty I pray, and that unborn fetus be granted the life, given by God, to live.

Thank you.

VETO MY VOTE

VETO MY VOTE
Vetar mi Voto
INTERMISSION

26 | Happy Pill

No one tells you that the side effect of having an abortion is depression. Shame, a very raw, acute and distressing feeling lingers. We experience shame when we are humiliated by our own sinful behavior. No, no one tells you that you're going to need a big dose of Happy Pill.

The whole scene is depressing, the clinic, the process, the procedure and the results. And the thoughts of what, where, how and what do they do with all that living matter which they suck and pull from your body. Where does it go. How do they suck from you life, leaving in its stead grief? After thoughts can be brutal.

If I had a flower to give for each procedure, I would give not to the Mom but just as a symbol of that child's cry to live.

27 | Not Even a Name

*The death of a loved one
can hit with so much pain.*

*News of the death
comes with so much grief and regret.*

*That happens when you love someone.
You don't want to see them leave.*

*Don't want to see them go.
Don't want to say bye-bye.*

*But what percentage of those good-byes do
a helpless Angel get?*

*Not even a name, or a grave to mark them
being in this world and the urgent exit
causing them to leave in a hurry.*

VETO MY VOTE

A lack of acknowledgment
seems all that's needed,
to let go of the memory.

No one to call Mom,
cause Mom's grief and regret just got
replaced by lust and shame.

Lust causing regret,
And Grief fades away to shame.

28 | Lust Baby

If the truth be told, there is a lot of lust babies being born into the world. What else would you call a love affair that didn't make it to the second date?

So, when lust comes into play, void of love and romance, only waiting to score points in the bedroom, deceiving the very elect, only to deselect and reject the offspring from this trumped-up affair, a fling. If it was a true love affair, we will be calling the offspring the love child.

29 | The Gift

A baby is a gift from God,
to be wanted and it demonstrates a mother's love to mankind,
how special and unique.

A mother's love demonstrated on the Earth is special.
God places it high on His list of all kinds of love.

A mother's love teaches lessons God will never have to teach
and shows the receiver of that love genuine love.

It shows each of us who receives a mother's love affection,
and caring so tender, and so special.

So, when the gift comes to you,
know that God is watching.

30 | Silent Playgrounds

When children are being gunned down on the streets of our
civilized cities every day, like shoot'em up in an old western film.

Silent playgrounds, evidence to an increasing number of the lost.
Headline news report a continual incline.

Cries, of which include mother's tears, loved ones and society.
We're crying because of the lost, we hear the silence.

News reports, everyday a different drama.
Mothers pleading for killers to turn themselves in.

Police search and active makeshift memorials.
Whose son, whose daughter today, we've had enough!

VETO MY VOTE

When we kill our unborn children,
a permanent termination, stopping their growth.

You just got to know you're working
on the side of the murderers of our youth.

31 | The Big

Thumbs Up

The murders of our unborn,
   No one to blame
      No one to accuse
         When the law books gave
         Thumbs up, a big O.K.
            Essentially permission was given

Now women line up
   To get their child aborted
      They line up to murder the seed
      Sprouting in their bellies
         To extinguish a birth and
         To reverse, a change of plans

VETO MY VOTE

Lessons learned when you raise a child
    Twenty-one years of mothership plus
        Everything negative that comes with having a child
        But everything positive also.

32 | *Popular Vote*

There was a time that I believed in the politicians that we elected into office. The truth is, that anytime you result to lying, it makes you unfit for the office as a politician. People do not like to be lied to. Many of our old and older politicians tell a bunch of them… to stay in office.

I believed that they spoke up for the people and steered government, law makers and future votes because of a true sense of concern. Only now to find out that these politicians only echo the concerns of a majority, pulling in their direction to receive a vote.

But there is more to politics than voting. We a population of people may cast our vote in favor of the candidate who we think can get a particular task done. And because societies have problems, let's cast our vote on he or she who can and will get the job done.

Let's agree also on what are society's problems and see if a politician's agenda line up with what we need as a society.

VETO MY VOTE

The more I reside on this Earth, the more I see that my concerns are not everyone else's concerns. My emergency is not my neighbor's emergency. But the concern of our youth should be every one's concern. Simply because our youth equates to our future.

So many old and older politicians. We know the common pros and cons surrounding topics of concern. Be honest with us, politicians, but most of all, be honest with yourself. Help us to see the fire in your eyes concerning the subject at hand. Don't just agree with it because you see a popular majority agreement. Sell to us why you agree or don't agree for that matter. How exactly are you going to fight for us? What makes you different from the next man, woman?

33 | *All Lives Matter*

I would like to take a moment to examine the catchy slogan,
"All Lives Matter" As opposed to "Black Lives Matter."
People use these catchy slogans
and really don't mean a word of it;
it just sounds good.

Do you really think for one moment, when people came up with "Black Lives Matter," that it was just a catchy phase? No. In a season where so many men of color, Black men are being killed in the streets, people who use that phase really do mean it. Not that all lives don't matter, but emphases were put on "Black Lives Matter" because   of the alarming rate in which people where being killed. But now in reexamining the slogan "All Lives Matter" I'm seeing that special importance should be given to children, particularly babies. How can you say, "All Lives Matter" and neglect attention to the rate in which the unborn murders are being covered up?

34 | What Did You Get from It?

Whenever you throw away something, it moves you sometimes because of the joy, or service, you got from it. You might even think twice before throwing it away. So, my question to you is what did you get from it?

Today we can recycle just about anything, from aluminum, to plastic, to newspapers and even compost for the farmer's soil. On your own, you might think of another way to use something as opposed to throwing it away, I do it all the time.

When a soul dies, it is laid to rest, given a descent funeral, pictures, dates of entrance and exit from Earth, individual contributions, host of relatives all included in the write up about his/her life. It is

our custom to dress the individual up, view his remains, even
honor him/her with flowers, and kind words in a gathering of
people who knew him/her most.

Many things we give to others when we no longer want them,
to a Good Will Store as a donation, or to a shelter,
or to family and friends.

We can think of millions of ways to reuse items we no longer want
or need. But how cruel to disregard the life of a child who has not
been given the rights to prove his/her worth.

Have you ever scribbled words on a piece of paper, then because
you've had a change in your thought process, ripped the paper
from the binder which held it? Then balled the paper up and with
the force of fury, threw it in the garbage. This is what that aborted
child's life meant to you. Accent on "ripped from the binder," and
"force of fury."

How can we as women continue to be defined in such a way?
I've always believed in women politicians because,
I thought they had a softer heart.
Has anyone ever told you that
there are two ways to solve a problem?
Yes, there is the hard way and the softer way.

Let it be clear that we all know how to
solve problems the hard way – like long division.
Or simply take a calculator
and solve the problem (soft way).

But let's look at some of the real problems in the world:
world peace, hunger, teen aged pregnancy, gun violence, hatred
(prejudice).

Sticking to our topic,
let's take teen pregnancy.

VETO MY VOTE

Do you really think solving this problem is to allow abortion?
That is like putting a band aid on the cut.
The cut that's bleeding profusely
and the wound is infected and stinking.
It's an excuse, a cop out,
a **way** out for society to continue to solve this problem this way.

It's a way to hide behind your back an evil truth.
It's a defeat to some when you continue to hide,
causing shame from deeds so easily acquired,
spreading blood on the hands of us all.

The true answer,
train them up;
the teen mom,
the unwanted little babe,
yes, even society to a better way.

The Police department have special equipment that they can see,
using this device when blood was attempted to be cleaned up.
So do the spirit as he told Cain

The voice of thy brother's blood
crieth unto me from the grave.
Genesis 4:8-11

35 | First Born

Even the Bible place emphasis on the first-born child in a family. Kings and Queens lay strict importance that an inheritance be given to a first-born child. There is a birth right to a first born.

So, where are our first-born children? They lay in the valley of the unborn. The bottom of the sea washed out to lay undeveloped in the bottom of the ocean. Our first born are being thrown away. But as they are being sucked out of their nesting place, its like a part of them scratch the surface. Like a hint to the next child in that spot that they were there. And the second child is born into the Earth's atmosphere. Given permission by his/her Mom to be born. Then comes into the world with a "knowing." A little extra knowledge about something he/she will never talk about, yet it becomes the foundation of their character.

The question is, "Do you think a child knows when there was a child before them in the womb?" Does a man know when he was not the first to penetrate the vaginal? Does a husband know if his wife cheated and had an affair while he was away? Who can truly say? Can a true mother look beyond words uttered or unuttered to see the real matter concerning her child? These are matters of the heart. I guess the real question is, "Can you read the heart of those close to you?"

A first-born child was there during the birth of all the others. Regardless if it's a man child or a girl, they are protective, humble, caring and seeing it first in their mother's eyes as she is caring for them both, and they are nurturers. These characteristics make good citizens. As they grow, their siblings give them strength. Some things in the world may scare them but they gain courage from their siblings. So, the family in that matter is balanced out. A first born is admired and looked upon for advice and direction or help and guidance. They are also often looked upon enviously and may never know why.

First born children of the world are truly unique individuals. But because of options to terminate a pregnancy with valid reasons like:
- Fear of the unknown that comes with rearing children, and the lack.
- The fears of new beginnings that comes with the struggles of life.
- An easy way out, changing the whole course and direction of life to those involved.
- And because of a system of women who have chosen this cause to be the fight which they have chosen to define them.

First born children are gentle giants because they experience early in life how to share. First born children go through some challenges where the other members in the family get away with, in fact they are the first to meet with these challenges such as:

- Tying shoes
- School
- Met with responsibilities
- Having keys, phone
- Taking siblings back and forth to school

Seems that first born children are equipped with knowledge of taking charge. They have seen some things because the eye of their intellect is turned on and they operate in teaching mode while still in learning mode. They are undercover agents in life, learning to abase and abound simultaneously. I know because I am a first-born child, having the heart of a first born.

36 | Wicked People in The Universe

These are the days where the rich, those who already have claimed enough money to hand down to their children and their children's children and looking for more and more. A day where although rich, greed has set in and is leading a sinister plan to hop on board of anything that will add more dollars to their swelling bank accounts. Where the wicked and sinister working together with a mad scientist to devise a plan to bring your unborn fetus to term.

That bothers me because undocumented people in the hands of evil, rich, and greedy people open the door to master mind slavery. It also opens up a new class of people in places where the law was not meant to go.

Child, you better think about this, think about it now as that baby swells in your belly. Do you not know that your unborn fetus could become the next generation of slaves? That scientists are already doing things that's against natural occurrences. Think about cross breeding, men and women taking shutter flights to and from the moon, next Mars? Think about cross gender and suppose I don't want to be no gender at all, or worse, both. Think about Frankenstein, now what was that all about?

People, we don't know what we're opening the door to. We don't know the ending of this story. But pray God's will be done.

37 | *Head vs. Heart*

Thinking about this using the head:

Visualizing a certain right that grants you the permission
to kill and destroy a fetus unborn will
never get the job done.

You got to consider this with your heart:

With the heart as we examine this issue,
it's called compassion.

38 | DNA Matters

We can have some doubts about who the father is in a child's birth. But how did we get to the place where a baby's birth mother is not his/her mother?

When DNA don't line up to support mother nor father it blows forensic science all the way up.

Most would say that you can't fight science and you would agree that when the facts line up, there is no denying.

We are making some left turns about how babies are born and who they are born to.

39 | You Might Say I'm Just Old

What race of people out there who can't learn
From the old generation?

What wisdom is there in your youth?

How wise can a young person be?

If the council of an older and wiser person can save
You from making a major mistake in life
Wouldn't you welcome it?

Who is the person who thinks they know everything?

Didn't you know that mistakes are meant to be learned from?

Mistakes teaches you something.
When you don't learn from your mistakes,
You will live to repeat that mistake.

The smart thing to do is to learn from the mistakes of others. So, listen to those old folks who have made a lot of mistakes in life.

They may not be rich, but they are full of wisdom and knowledge.

40 | Treason

Somebody call treason
When a nation is being stolen
　　When the Prince of the air has deceived
　　　　Women who believe in their hearts and mind
　　　　　　That they are doing the right thing to
　　　　　　　　Destroy their unborn children.

Treason, somebody need to say
Exactly the crime of Pharaoh
　　Tried to kill the baby Jesus
　　　　And Joseph being warned in a dream
　　　　　　Or the baby Moses
　　　　　　　　Escaped only to be raised
　　　　　　　　　　By the King's own sister.

It's a trick I tell you, and I am sounding the alarm
T R E A S O N.

You're responsible for a monarch that will
Not be born if you throw that seed away.
　　It's a trick and I'm shouting TREASON.

41 | Sperm Donor

You give the world a tube full of seeds
  Frozen against time
    To come forth at the hour of need

True fathers of the world, give us your seeds
  Thrust forward now
    At the coming of a great release

The one present when there is a need
  The other unavoidable during passions of love

VETO MY VOTE

The tube full of seeds, should everyone be used
   Can a man, doctor, or anyone
      Know which to choose

As in passions of love, a great number released
   Only one to penetrate the egg
      Maybe two in the birth of twins

True fathers of the world, give us your seeds
   Thrust forward now
      At the coming of a great release

42 | Once Upon a Time

THERE WAS ONCE A BLACK MAN, ISADORE BANKS.
He was a man of enterprise, worked hard, owned farms and land.
He was in business, and he prospered greatly.
One day this prosperous Black man came up missing.

The headlines read:

Arkansas Slaying Of Farmer A Legacy Vanished
"Burned, Tied Body of a Negro is Founded in Marion Vicinity,"
        Arkansas Gazette, June 10, 1954, p. 1B
"Chain Arkansas Farmer to Tree, Set Him Afire,"
        Chicago Defender, June 26, 1954, p. 5
"Chained to Tree, Burned to Death,"
        Pittsburgh Courier, June 19, 1954, p. 1
Charred Body is Still a Mystery,"

VETO MY VOTE

Arkansas State Press, June 18, 1954, p. 1
"Negro Death is Believed Murder,"
Crittenden County Times, June 12, 1954, p. 1

Isadore Banks, fifty-nine years old, prominent African-American landowner, disappeared on June 4, 1954.

Despite obstacles, Banks had become a prominent and respected leader, a Freemason, and one of the wealthiest African-American landowners in the region of Arkansas. Banks is reported to own more than 1,000 acres of land which he farmed or leased to tenants, and several businesses. Banks helped other Black farmers with loans to buy seeds and farm equipment and supported the local Black school with supplies.

This is what happens when a seed is murdered.

43 | Team

I know a man whom I consider a close friend.
He has learned some hard lessons in life,
But the fact is he has learned from his mistakes.
These lessons have caused him to live his children bearing years behind bars.

Now back out in society he's still learning some lessons.
Now the man is above all, a very hard-working man.
He has built a business making people's front and back lawns pretty,
Beautiful, growing the way that God had intended.
As his business grows, he is finding a need to have people work with him.
Now this is the part that would have benefitted him,
If perhaps he had some children to help build the team he needs.

**Which is the very same thing that happens when we abort
our children.**
Sometimes the type of work we do will involve a team,
Something that we will not be able to accomplish on our own.
**So, we need our off springs, the availability of strong and
able minds and bodies.**

Who can deny that a child, flesh of your own flesh
Would make a great team member.

**If your plans involve building a brand, entrepreneurship,
owning a business,
Who can deny your teaching your own children first hand
To become the leadership in something you create.**

44 | Throw Away Child

I once met a young man. When I asked him what his name was, he told me, "Throw Away Child." I told him that I could not call him that. There was bogged down anger in him because his Mom abandoned him and went on with her life, left him with Dad. Which is the same thing she did with other children she allowed access into the Earth.

The many children that we abandon when we abort, don't carry the child to term, or murder by sucking the child out of the womb. These children we will see again. They have souls and when they are killed, their little spirits ascend back up to the giver of life.

And God, who already knows the story, reveal a little humor, saying, "Wait a minute, didn't I just dispatch you to be born?" Then assigns the soul to Kiddy Heaven. These are the souls without a story for their life on Earth. Which was truly only a few months.

VETO MY VOTE

So, when the Mom this child was dispatched to appears before the judgment gate, the little soul shows up to introduce themselves, and confront Mom, pleading why, oh why did you abandon me. And God will hear the story, the why, how, and what happened to this gift which was given to you. The gift that you littered as trash back into the atmosphere. But not only that, you Mom will hear the whole story of what God intended for this soul's life to become.

...Only God will judge Moms everywhere... But who will you call on to justify your decision in this matter?

45 | *Crimes in Law*

The Voice of Blood Cries Out,
Blood-soaked America:

The Blood of the African man
His legacy, his history, generations upon
Generations, an unjust defeat
Now the struggle upwards and onwards unjust also.

The Blood of the unborn
The murder of countless
Laws of permits amongst promiscuity,
Random and irresponsibility seeking to hide behind laws
The shame yet do it again and again.
Learning nothing, gaining nothing, contributing nothing.

Saying and protecting the right of the people
To keep and bear arms, guns, ammunitions
And the stores where they are sold. For what is a gun

VETO MY VOTE

Without ammunition, used to attack,
Leaving the life of defenseless victims against a fire,
An explosion, from such a weapon.

Knowing all too well that these things are not in the will
nor plan of God the Father of man. As it is written in the
Bible, "Thou shall not kill," in the ten commandments. Yet
fathers of the laws of this country include as law. This
America has been divided since the days of slavery. States
that practiced slave trading and states which were against
it. But ending slave trading did not end our indifference but
started yet another struggle for the Black man.

This divided nation will be its own defeat. For the woes do
come, one behind the other. Famine and sickness, torn in
the stance of Roe v Wade, people have taken to the streets
to voice their opinion, but not just their opinion, their dire
hopes and desires, now mass shootings in peaceful towns,
same race crimes toward society, toward innocent victims,
and even wars, and the threats of wars to come, grows rage.

Yes, the division has caused a rage and the rage
Is growing and growing to condom hate
And hate grows to murder, producing more rage.
It's like a marriage made in hell and rage is the offspring,
The child if you will of such a marriage.

We look at the war in Ukraine like it's the worst thing,
Yet we hide our hands at the war we face daily here in
front yards Center stage crimes in law.

46 |

Heaven's Check in Gate

After the souls of countless unborn
The soul of a soldier checked in
The soul of a man heavy
    He looked tired and worn
        And with a beard down to his belly.

Many times, as souls line up
    You'll hear often times of the fight
        The struggle at Earth's battlefield.

You'll hear if you listen
    The true intent of the soul's hope
        You'll hear the accusations against him
            And his testimony you'll hear.

VETO MY VOTE

While a host of angels
  Appear before this soul
    With one job and one job only
      To judge this soul and deem him righteous
        Or give him a one-way ticket straight to HELL.

Many come with their made-up stories
  Bearing false witness
    As the accusers cry out against them
      You threw me away, I had no life because of you
        Will your reasons why line up when you are standing
        At the judgement gate?

These are the souls that would be surprised
  At that great getting up morning
    The ones whose intent was to make it to heaven
      And missed it by a hair.

The moment of their transgression
  Brought up in their mind's eye
    Giving them to relive their thoughts
      Their actions and the self-righteous moments in their life.
Then their accusers flood their mind
  With a glimpse of what it would have been like
    Had they chosen to give the child a life
      Rather than abort.

Choice is a powerful liberty
  That can be clouded by thoughts of self-righteousness
    Choice can give you the world in life
      But that same choice can deem you
        Unfit to enter the Kingdom of Heaven.

When the question comes to the soul of the unborn
  Where are the hands of them who caused your life to end?

Hounds at My Feet

Thank you, Father, for catching me when you did.
I escaped the forces of darkness and did run to escape.

I heard them talking about it, planning my demise,
like I was some big threat.

I heard them making preparations, felt Mom's heartbeat as my
heart did beat in unison.

Then did they tug at my feet, in my spirit,
I put up a fight, and then it was over.

Thank you, Father, for catching me when you did.
I escaped the forces of darkness and did run to escape for the
hounds were at my feet.

48 | Woman, Be True to Yourself

If women would just find themselves
  And see that God has a plan for your life
- Your team
  And if you raise them up right,
- Even your mistakes

What the Devil meant for bad
- God will make your joy

If you learn from your mistakes
- Then teach those growing up under you
- To avoid these same mistakes

VETO MY VOTE

Then will you prosper
-     Then will we all prosper

Turn from your wicked ways
-     Pray and seek the face of God
-     Then will He hear you from heaven

49 | I Want to Live

I want to live!

     Live to jump rope.
     Live to ride my bike.

     Live to go to school.
     Live to make friends.

I want to live!

     Live to see the warmth of a sunset.
     Live to see a sandy shoreline.

     Live to see stars in the sky.
     Live to see a rainbow.

I want to live!

     Live to dream.
     Live to have siblings.

     Live to embrace my Mom.
     Live to serve you in praise and worship
          And to bring in a mighty number, into salvation.

50 |  Mistakes...

When a person learns from a mistake.
We can say, "That was a lesson well learned,"
But when you don't learn from your mistakes,
And live to repeat the mistake over and over again
It begins to be a cop out.

You can say it was a mistake
   Can't say you're sorry
      You might even say it's done purposely.

When you erase a word on your paper,
You replace it with a better word
A more intended word.

How about learning from someone else mistakes.
Wise people will talk about their mistakes for that purpose,
To keep others from going down the rabbit's hole.
To help others learn the same exact lesson needed to do better.

Mistakes are a natural part of growing up.
Watching children in this process,
They will repeat a thing over and over until they get it right.

It is their goal to get it right,
    To do it the way others do it successfully
        To be satisfied themselves with the finish product.

It should be in our DNA to be successful in our growing.

Acknowledgments

First and foremost, I'd like to thank God for allowing me to go through my journey of life in which I have been able to learn and grow from my circumstances, and change my challenges into this beautiful work of art and book series of poems.

And to my mother, Leola Reynolds, whom told the best stories when I was growing up. My love for her and her stories as she told us as we were growing up were quite splendid.

And to my readers, I am grateful for your support I'd like to offer some wisdom. When an older person has a story to tell, sit down and listen because it will be a good story, one of true wisdom.

About the Author

Born to Gentle Frank Fields and Leola Reynolds, Pamela Fields grew up on the south side of Chicago, Illinois, where she attended several elementary schools and Wendell Phillips High School, all schools located in Chicago, Illinois. She also attended Harold Washington Junior College and would go on to major is Early Childhood Education. She later attended Prestige Nurse Aide Training Academy, where she attained her certification as a CNA. Both of the selected majors were encouraged by her experiences of not wanting any child to be left behind, nor any older adult left uncared for.

Fields held the position of being the oldest of her siblings, one sister, and two brothers. She refers to her brothers and sister as stair-steps as each sibling is one year apart from the other. Fields acknowledge her siblings and Richard Reynolds, her superhero and second husband to her mother, for preparing her to understand and learn several tactics of dealing with the way of the world. Fields has three children: Nikia Fields, Edward Fields, and Shana Edwards, and she loves them all dearly. Her children have blessed her with eight grandchildren, and Fields continues to shower them with the educational packages from her homemade learning lessons.

Getting into the professional side of life, Fields was employed at several early learning centers. She also worked as a CNA on weekends, and she spent a few evening hours taking care of her mother. Her years of employment with others have led her to her Happily Ever After, becoming a future best-selling author with S.H.E. PUBLISHING LLC, and starting up two businesses simultaneously, one being K.I.N.D.N.E.S.S. Kare (*Keys IN Developing & Navigating Effective Social Solutions*), a childcare service, and Pam's Baking Handz.

Ultimately, Fields purpose and passion is to bring together ordinary people like you and me with the commitment to encourage us to love one another. She believes that it's the small efforts of a friendly smile, the gift of gratitude, praying for one another, and small acts of kindness that will change the world one day, one hour, and one second at a time. It only takes a second to yield a smile and patience doesn't cost anything.

Thanks for reading!
Please add a short review on
Amazon and S.H.E. PUBLISHING LLC.
Let me know your thoughts!